X 363.32
BAKER, DAVID
Infiltration & spying.

D1411141

INFILTRATION & SPYING

FIGHTING TERRORISM

David Baker

ST. CHARLES PARISH LIBRARY
105 LAKEWOOD DRIVE
P.O. BOX 949
LULING, LA 70070

© 2006 Rourke Publishing LLC
All rights reserved. No part of this book may be reproduced or utilized in any form or by any means, electronic or mechanical including photocopying, recording, or by any information storage and retrieval system without permission in writing from the publisher.

www.rourkepublishing.com

PHOTO CREDITS: p. 10: Yasser Al-Zayyat/AFP/Getty Images; p. 39: AnwarAmro/AFP/Getty Images; pp. 18, 19 (b): Corbis; p. 32: Corbis Sygma; pp. 25, 35: Department of Defense; p. 34: Discovery Books Ltd; p. 12: Getty Images; p. 11: Chris Hondros/Getty Images; p. 40: Hulton Archive/Getty Images; p. 8: Paul Humphrey/Chris Fairclough Worldwide Ltd; pp. 21, 23: Imperial War Museum; p. 15: Keystone/Getty Images; pp. 19 (t), 20: Library of Congress; p. 29: John MacDougall/AFP/Getty Images; p. 30: Motorola; p. 14: Norbain SD Ltd; p. 43: Scott Peterson/Getty Images; p. 5: Edy Purnomo/Getty Images; p.17: RDA/Tallandier/Getty Images; p. 41: Reuters/Corbis; p. 13: Stortech Electronics Ltd; pp. 24 (Master Sgt. Jim Varhegyi), 31 (Joe Mekina), 33 (Carleton Bailie): U.S. Air Force; p. 7 (Staff Sgt. Joseph P. Collins Jr.): U.S. Army; p. 37 (Lance Cpl. Justin M. Mason): U.S. Marine Corps; pp. 6 (Seaman David P. Coleman), 27 (Photographer's Mate 2nd Class Todd Reeves): U.S. Navy; p. 26: Tim Wright/Corbis

Title page picture shows a satellite photograph of a terrorist training camp in Afghanistan.

Produced for Rourke Publishing by Discovery Books
Editor: Paul Humphrey
Designer: Ian Winton
Photo researcher: Rachel Tisdale

Library of Congress Cataloging-in-Publication Data

Baker, David, 1944-
  Infiltration and spying / by David Baker.
      p. cm. -- (Fighting terrorism)
  Includes index.
  ISBN 1-59515-486-8
  1. Terrorism--Prevention--Juvenile literature. 2. Espionage--Juvenile literature. 3. Infiltration (Military science)--Juvenile literature. I. Title. II. Series.
  HV6431.B335 2006
  363.320973--dc22

                                        2005028009

Printed in the USA

TABLE OF CONTENTS

Chapter One

Ways to Fight Terrorism

Fighting terrorism is as important a part of national defense as are the fighting forces that protect U.S. interests in peace and war. Terrorism is not new. It is as old as nations, and it will always be with us. This is because, just as there are always people who will commit criminal acts in our society, there will always be those who seek to achieve by violence the things they cannot achieve by persuasion in the global community.

Terrorism is practiced by people who put their political or **ideological** loyalties above care and concern for human life. It takes place when tolerance and compassion are replaced by fanaticism and hate. Terrorism results in violence and murder through attacks on innocent people usually unknown to the assassins but who are condemned by the beliefs terrorists hold. Because of that it is intolerable and cannot be allowed to succeed.

The fight against terrorism employs several government agencies, each one specialized in a particular field of operation. The Department of Homeland Security coordinates anti-terrorism activities through a wide range of different

The aftermath of the terrorist bombing on the Indonesian island of Bali, on October 12, 2002, which left hundreds of tourists and local people dead or injured.

government departments. The Department of State looks after our relations with other nations in the battle against international terror. The Department of Defense strikes at organized groups or countries that support terrorism and who use it against us and our allies.

Detection of terrorists, **liaisons** with other countries in the never-ending war against acts of violence, and the response we

In the fight against terror it is important that our government and its agencies react and respond in a lawful manner. Sometimes fighting terrorism seems to conflict with the rights of the individual. In the United States the basic right to assume innocence until guilt is proven is an important part of responding to terrorism in a responsible and civilized manner.

can make depends on what we know and where we look to get the information essential to preventing further attacks. It is all about **intelligence** and about **infiltrating** the gangs and the bands of criminals that practice terrorism. This means that sometimes we have to spy on our enemies to keep them from carrying out their vicious intentions.

Camp Delta in Guantanamo Bay, Cuba, serves as a temporary holding facility for terrorist suspects. Some people question whether the United States should be holding people who have not been indicted for an offense.

Chapter Two

Bugs and Infiltrators

Any good military commander knows that the way to win a war is to have three essential assets. He must have effective weapons, a disciplined fighting force, and adequate logistics and

A soldier from the Virginia National Guard stoops to enter and search the home of a suspected Taliban member in Afghanistan on June 4, 2005. Good intelligence is crucial if our troops are to know where to look for the enemy.

A street market in Chicago. Terrorists can hide anywhere and look just like ordinary people. This makes them very hard to detect.

good information about the enemy. Information, or intelligence, is gathered from a wide variety of sources. During most wars the enemy is known and all too obvious. The enemy can be identified as a recognizable force with visible weapons and ammunition, usually comes with a uniform, and almost always belongs to a specific country.

The war against terrorism is very different. The enemy is disguised, the terrorist choosing to blend into the crowd or hide so as not to be detected. These enemies do not belong to a particular country or to an easily identifiable group. This unique problem of recognizing the enemy is a difficulty for defense forces that only special recognition techniques can overcome.

Terrorists choose to hide their identity because they operate outside the agreed rules of engagement to which most countries around the world have pledged their support. Generally, in past wars, acts of aggression against an armed force conducted by people without uniform or a recognizable flag were considered outside the rule of law.

FACT FILE ★

Agreements about the conduct of troops in war were first drawn up in a document known as the Geneva Convention of 1864. This has subsequently been modified and added to with rules and regulations concerning the proper way to use force in war. It was created in the year that the city of Geneva in southeast Switzerland— traditionally a neutral country—became the headquarters for the International Red Cross.

Such people have been treated as spies or terrorists (sometimes referred to as **guerrillas**) and tried under military law. This has often resulted in a death sentence. Most countries, therefore, agree that such action is illegal according to international law. Attacks against civilians by such groups are against civil law, and attacks by such people against troops are against agreed military law.

Because terrorists have no means of being easily recognized, it is necessary to use unusual means to gather information about their whereabouts, the groups they form into, the places where they live and train, and the methods they use to

Members of Al Qaeda at a training camp in Afghanistan. Al Qaeda operates in remote places where it is difficult to infiltrate the organization.

communicate with each other. It is a technical challenge to combat their destructive intentions and one that uses all the resources of modern warfare.

Modern technology is a great tool when fighting terrorist groups, but none is more important than the most sophisticated asset of all—the well-trained spy. Highly trained specialists capable of gaining access to information networks, working their way into secret terrorist groups or gathering information by placing "bugs" in the right place, provide the vital information for fighting these outlaws. People who gain the confidence of terrorist groups and report to intelligence organizations about their activities and plans are known as infiltrators.

When it comes to fighting terrorism, all the weapons in the world are not equal to the value obtained from one good intelligence-gathering human. High-tech weapon systems can dig out tunnels and caves occupied by gangs of terrorists in remote mountain regions in a far-off country, but bugs and infiltrators provide a vital link to the thoughts and intentions of these unpredictable outlaws.

Al Qaeda terrorists hid in caves in the Tora Bora region of Afghanistan, where the placing of bugs was almost impossible.

Chapter Three

The Role of Spies

Spies have played a vital role in intelligence gathering for as long as there have been groups of people suspicious of each other's intentions. They are even mentioned in the Bible, where, after succeeding Moses to leadership of the Children of Israel, Joshua sent spies to survey the land of Canaan "flowing with milk and honey." In almost all wars since those far-off days, when the world's first great civilizations were being formed, intelligence gathering has been an essential part of preparing proper defenses and understanding the enemy.

Tiny video cameras and bugging devices can be hidden almost anywhere. This smoke detector contains a tiny video camera.

In the modern world there are many ways in which information can be obtained without having to infiltrate countries or groups considered dangerous. The human brain, still far more sophisticated and capable than the most powerful computer on earth, can make decisions and judgments important to the fight against terrorism. When equipped with technical aids and devices able to gather

*(Opposite) Denise Richards with Pierce Brosnan as James Bond in **The World Is Not Enough**. In reality the world of the spy is quite different than that shown in the movies.*

information the human cannot, the combination is powerful.

The spy today can be a special agent traveling in disguise or a technical specialist gathering information from different sources. Or, the modern spy can be a computer operator accessing coded communication channels or an analyst working with information gathered from a satellite in space.

CCTV cameras like this one helped to catch suspected terrorists who tried to blow up parts of the London subway system in July 2005.

The special agent operating in a foreign country or infiltrating a dangerous group of terrorists puts his or her life on the line all the time. If caught, there is no mercy. Unprotected by any law, spies are on their own and are usually disowned by the country for whom they work. This is because conventional rules of engagement between armed forces in war do not protect spies. Because they must blend in with the rest of the population, spies operate without uniform with the object of gaining secret information about a foreign country.

During the Cold War that emerged between the United States and the Soviet Union after World War II ended in 1945, many spies were caught and shot. By that time there had been a long history of intelligence gathering and for good reason.

When the communists took over Russia after the October 1917 revolution they promised to export terror and revolution around the world. They murdered the rulers of Russia and set up a **totalitarian** state in which leaders were chosen among a group of top communists without real democratic elections and without **opposition parties** to challenge their decisions.

Julius Rosenberg (shown here) and his wife, Ethel, were arrested as Soviet spies in July 1950, at the height of the Cold War. They were convicted and executed on June 19, 1953.

Because they thought people in capitalist democratic countries should be "liberated" from control by those people who employed them, the Soviets began a campaign to support revolutionary and terrorist organizations around the world.

During the 1950s the Soviets encouraged freedom fighters in other countries to carry out acts of terrorism against their rulers. These countries included Indonesia, China, Vietnam, Korea, and Pakistan among others. By carrying out bombings, burnings, and killings, they roused a few supporters and put fear into the majority of decent citizens. In many countries affected by terrorists, gangs of outlaws created havoc and panic that led to governments being overthrown by riots and fear.

In some cases the new rulers who promised peace were paid by the terrorists, the people believing they would be getting governments that would stop the terror. They were, but unknown to the public it was a means of putting

FACT FILE ★

Terrorists who fight against oppression in their own countries are sometimes called **freedom fighters**, but that title has now been taken by desperate groups of fanatical **extremists** who carry out murder and bombings in other countries. By adopting this phrase they seek, unsuccessfully, to bring a respectable purpose to their acts of violence. Freedom fighters struggle against dictators and tyrant rulers in their own countries. Terrorists attack the innocent to create fear and panic in an attempt to put pressure on other countries to carry out their demands.

leaders in power already selected by the terrorists and paid by them to carry out their demands. It was against this background that the United States built up a **credible** network of spies and intelligence specialists that formed the front line against terrorism.

People in the French Resistance were freedom fighters. They fought against the Germans who occupied their country during World War II (1939-1945). Most modern terrorists are not freedom fighters.

Chapter Four

Spy Schools

The origins of U.S. intelligence and its network of spies and agents go back to the dark days of World War II when, on December 7, 1941, Japan attacked naval forces at Pearl Harbor,

Hawaii. President Franklin D. Roosevelt recognized that America needed much better intelligence information to assist its military forces in achieving victory, and he set up several organizations to get that. He formed the Office of Strategic Services, the OSS, to carry out **sabotage** in enemy-occupied countries, to conduct intelligence operations, and to gather details about enemy forces.

This was the first real experience American spies had of working in foreign countries to gather information vital to success. The Army and the Navy had their own intelligence services and used this information to learn about enemy troop and naval movements as they

Soon after Pearl Harbor, President Franklin D. Roosevelt (above) set up the Office of Strategic Services with Allen W. Dulles (right) at its head.

(Opposite) The attack on Pearl Harbor on December 7, 1941, brought the United States into World War II and led to the setting up of the U.S. intelligence service.

were happening, thereby avoiding the shock of a surprise attack.

Shortly after victory was achieved in 1945, President Harry S. Truman set up the Central Intelligence Agency, the CIA. When in 1947 the U.S. Air Force became independent from the Army, all three armed services had their own spy networks gathering intelligence vital for land, sea, and air forces.

President Harry S. Truman was responsible for setting up the Central Intelligence Agency when he signed the 1947 National Security Act.

Coordinating defense operations and activities among all the forces, the Department of Defense created the Defense Intelligence Agency, the DIA, to gather strategic information vital to America's global defense interests.

With an increasingly hostile Soviet Union threatening to enforce communism wherever it could, the lessons of Pearl Harbor were not forgotten. America would best protect its people by never again underestimating the enemy and by always being prepared to defend itself against attack. Intelligence would be the key—as it is today—to preventing aggression and halting the attacks before they could start.

Intelligence networks need spies. The **recruitment** of agents in the late 1940s to infiltrate communist countries brought a need for the first U.S. **espionage** schools. The OSS had set up America's first spy schools in England during World War II with the cooperation of Great Britain's Special Operations Executive, or SOE. The SOE had been set up in 1940 by the British Secret Service and had the job of carrying out subversive activity in Nazi-occupied Europe.

At that time, Nazi-controlled Germany occupied mainland Europe from the French coast to the border with Russia. Great Britain wanted to disrupt Nazi operations and worked with freedom fighters in these occupied countries to liberate their

Special Operations Executive forces were dropped into enemy-occupied territory during World War II.

land from fascist oppression. When American forces went to Great Britain, the OSS trained its spies over there and at a special location in Canada known as Camp X. The spy schools of today are the most advanced of their kind in the world and have been built directly from those early days when much had to be learned that was essential to victory.

The CIA set up a spy school at Camp Peary, Virginia, and the FBI had a school at Quantico, Virginia, a large Marine Corps base. The FBI was interested in criminal law enforcement activities, and sometimes these skills were important for terrorist prevention. Working internally, the FBI would coordinate activities with the CIA, which was specifically involved with gathering information from outside the United States.

The army traditionally trained its intelligence specialists at a school in Fort Halobird in Baltimore, Maryland, nicknamed "The Bird," but it later moved to Fort Huachuca, Arizona. The Army, Navy, and Air Force have specialized training programs at places across the continental United States, and each service recruits volunteers from inside its own ranks for agents to

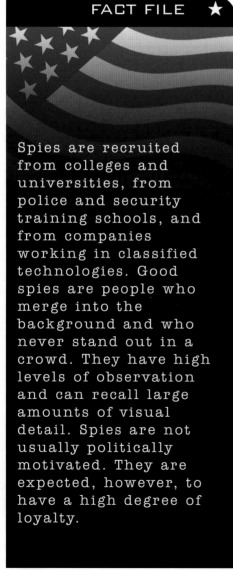

FACT FILE ★

Spies are recruited from colleges and universities, from police and security training schools, and from companies working in classified technologies. Good spies are people who merge into the background and who never stand out in a crowd. They have high levels of observation and can recall large amounts of visual detail. Spies are not usually politically motivated. They are expected, however, to have a high degree of loyalty.

Oluf Olsen, an SOE wireless operator, sits at his radio set deciphering an incoming message.

gather and interpret intelligence information. Linking all these services is the Joint Military Intelligence College at Bolling Air Force Base in Washington, D.C., an institution that works closely with the Defense Intelligence Agency and sometimes with the CIA.

Cooperation among the intelligence services is very important. Each has its own specialties, and working together increases their **efficiency**. Frequently it is necessary to interpret messages or to communicate in a different language. Sometimes agents must be skilled in speaking foreign languages fluently. Much intelligence gathering relies on picking up signals from foreign countries or groups talking to each other.

Foreign languages are taught at the Defense Language School in Monterey, California, and agents from all military services go

Soldiers from the 11th Communication Squadron at Bolling Air Force Base in Washington D.C. The base is home to the Joint Military Intelligence College.

A U-2 spy plane. The U-2, first used in the 1950s, is still at the forefront of intelligence gathering for the United States military. In June 2005, a U-2 crashed while on a surveillance mission over Afghanistan.

there to become fluent in specific languages. This is a vital part of any intelligence operation. Listening to conversations, chatter, instructions, messages, and general talk helps build a picture of activity difficult to get in any other way.

Today, the fight against terrorism uses advanced electronic eavesdropping equipment that has grown out of Cold War technology. When the Soviet Union posed a serious political and military threat, it was necessary to listen in to their communications. Equipment developed in those years of Cold War confrontation formed the basis for advanced listening systems now vital in the fight against terrorism.

One of the first major developments in Cold War intelligence operations was the gathering of information from radio signals. These carry voice traffic, coded messages, electronic information, and a variety of intelligence data sent between military units. The principal U.S. **electronic intelligence**-gathering organization was created in 1952, since then known as the National Security Agency, or NSA. It has its headquarters at Fort Meade, Maryland, and it is one of the most secret organizations in the U.S. arsenal of intelligence-gathering assets.

The Sugar Grove electronic surveillance facility in West Virginia is one of the NSA's top listening posts. From here, intelligence agents can tune in to phone calls, faxes, and e-mails from around the world.

The entire spectrum of **signals-intelligence** (sigint) information gathering is one of the most powerful tools available to the United States. It has stations not only throughout the United States but also in countries across the globe. The NSA is much larger than the CIA in terms of the number of people working for it and the budget it draws upon.

Estimates vary as to numbers, but it is believed nearly 40,000 people are employed by the NSA. People working for the organization receive information from electronic listening devices under the sea, on ships, on land, in the air, and in space. All this was developed as a result of potential threats from military aggression in the form of the Soviet Union between 1945 and 1990. Now it is one of the most important parts of the spy game—listening to conversations, intercepting messages, decoding encrypted messages, and much more.

Underwater listening devices are just one of the many tools available to the NSA. This picture shows U.S. Navy divers positioning an underwater listening device in the ocean near San Clemente Island, California.

Chapter Five

High-tech Spies in the Sky

Terrorists can operate as lone assassins or in organized groups coordinating a complicated attack. Sometimes they need special equipment, chemicals for bombs, technical information for making explosives, and detailed information about their targets. Organized use of money, fund raising, and the use of banks in sympathetic countries such as Libya require a steady flow of communications. Above all, the terrorists need to maintain silence and avoid detection.

This is difficult when communication is the way to get the essential ingredients for their activities. Telephone tapping, listening in to their telephone conversations, would give intelligence gatherers a head start in defeating their aims. The problem is that at any one time around the world there are more than 1 billion telephone conversations going on simultaneously involving 2 billion people! How to find the ones that matter? That is largely the job of the NSA—the signals intelligence specialists who must eavesdrop for signs of a plot.

Radio stations around the world operated by the NSA can listen in on people talking anywhere on earth. With the move

Libya's central bank in Tripoli. It is believed that, until recently, the Libyan government was financing terrorist groups around the world.

toward wireless communications, the widespread use of cell phones makes it much easier to trap terrorists. Radio signals that travel along wires are difficult to intercept by remote means. Cell phones connected by radio waves usually allow signals to be intercepted with ease.

Unlike the enemies of the Cold War, today's terrorists can hide in remote places and deserted regions far from developed or highly organized cities. There are difficulties with intercepting even cell phone traffic in and out of such places. Moreover, with current technology satellite telephones allow direct access to

Calls from cell phones are easier to intercept than those from traditional land lines.

people anywhere on earth. Today's terrorists are highly organized and have access to these devices. It is far easier to intercept these signals from space.

To do so the NSA listens in to different conversations from suspected terrorists using sensitive devices called **frequency-scanners**. Cell phones and satellite telephones use radio signals to connect people talking to each other. The radio channel used by the cell phone can be tapped by receivers tuned to the same frequency. The receiver is connected to a powerful antenna that collects the stray signals. To do so the scanners must be very sensitive because the strength of the signal is very weak.

Back in the days of the Cold War, satellites designed to collect telephone traffic got the name of electronic intelligence, or elint, satellites. Because the radio signals were very weak, the satellites were in low orbits, but with current technology they can be far out in space in **geostationary** orbit.

In geostationary orbit the satellite takes 24 hours to complete one orbit of the earth, exactly the same time it takes the earth to revolve once on its polar axis. Hence, the satellite appears to remain stationary. From this kind of orbit the satellite can appear

A Joined-wing Technology Demonstrator in flight in September 2004. When this high-tech airplane enters service, it will carry a mix of radar, cameras, and elint equipment.

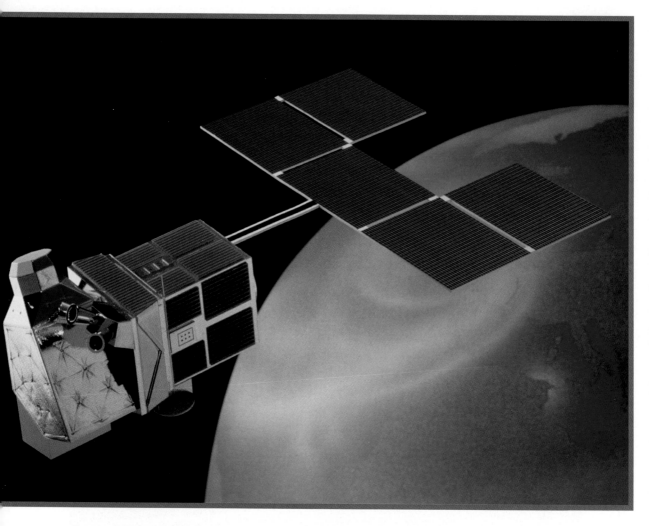

Spy satellites like the French Helios provide invaluable information on the communications and movements of terrorist groups.

to sit over one fixed position on earth and listen in continuously to telephone traffic going on below.

This is telephone tapping on a big scale and requires very powerful equipment. Consequently, elint satellites are very big and have enormous antennas. And they are very expensive. Fortunately they can do more than just pick up telephone traffic. They can also tap into e-mails and websites and dig out secret

A new spy satellite is launched from Cape Canaveral, Florida, joining the other high-tech "eyes and ears in the sky" that keep our country safe from terrorist attack.

Elint satellites can intercept e-mails and Internet traffic, as well as phone calls.

signals buried inside the main traffic. Anything that goes by radio signal can be intercepted from the ground, from the air, or from satellites in space.

Because an increasing amount of our total communications now goes by radio signals rather than by wire, it is easier to keep track of conversations. The NSA is prohibited by law from eavesdropping on calls in the United States. This is because of the Foreign Intelligence Surveillance Act, which has been interpreted to allow tapping of calls only where one end of the conversation is in the United States.

A satellite photograph of a terrorist training camp in a remote part of Afghanistan.

In days of extreme threat and danger from terrorists, this is considered by our representatives in Congress to be a wise interpretation of the law. However, calls outside the United States are monitored if they are likely to assist with the detection of international criminals or terrorists. In very remote places such as Afghanistan, where Al Qaeda still has hideouts and training camps, radio communication is the only way of getting information in or out of these secret locations.

There are added advantages. This is also a way of finding where the terrorists are hidden. When a terrorist switches on his satellite phone, the signal is detected by the NSA from its elint station in space. A few seconds of tracking gives the location of the caller. This has resulted in terrorists using high-tech equipment to avoid detection. The terrorist can do this by attaching a device to his telephone that continuously

FACT FILE ★

Ground stations and satellites are important assets when it comes to keeping track of telephone calls and e-mail messages between terror groups. Other tracking carriers are also used. U.S. forces in Afghanistan left sleeper-trackers buried in remote regions to which terrorists might return. These send out no signal to indicate their presence but work as **transponders**—only responding to a signal sent out from a cell phone or satellite phone nearby. When they "hear" that signal, they immediately send it via satellite or a patrolling aircraft and notify the intelligence operators that people are in the area and have switched on their telephones.

changes the frequency of the radio signal. This frequency-hopping technique confuses the tracker because the signal keeps changing.

It's like a radio station that continuously changes frequency—you have to keep turning the dial to find the new location of the station. So it is with the space tracker, except that it is more difficult because the device changes frequencies several times a second! The satellite does this too, continuously scanning up and down the full span of radio frequencies several hundred times a second continuously hunting down—and locking in—to the conversation. It is a constant game of cat and mouse.

U.S. forces in Afghanistan left high-tech bugging devices that can detect the presence of anyone in the area.

Chapter Six

Infiltrating the Enemy Camp

Keeping track of suspects and known terrorists is not only an important part of attack prevention, but it is also an important means of cutting off supplies and starving terrorists of funds. Terrorists need explosives, igniters, timers, fuses, arms, and plans of targets and attack points. By tracking their communications it is sometimes possible to hunt down their sources of supply. Techniques like these have been used to link some supply countries, even private companies, with terrorist groups.

For instance, the Irish Republican Army, the IRA, was the illegal militant arm of the political party Sinn Fein, which wanted unification of the Republic of Ireland (Southern Ireland) and the British territory of Ulster (Northern Ireland). IRA members were thought by some to be freedom fighters, but they behaved like terrorists because they maimed and killed innocent people in Great Britain and elsewhere.

In 1979, Lord Louis Mountbatten, cousin of British Queen Elizabeth II, was killed by terrorists from the IRA. The terrorists had been trained in the Soviet Union, and the operation, which involved a bomb aboard a fishing boat carrying Mountbatten,

Hezbollah is a notorious terrorist group operating against the state of Israel. Groups such as these are extremely difficult for western intelligence agents to infiltrate.

was carried out in a combined operation involving the KGB, the dreaded Soviet secret police.

In an attempt to kill the British Prime Minister Margaret Thatcher and her cabinet in 1984, IRA terrorist Patrick Magee planted a bomb in a hotel where they were staying, killing 5 people and injuring 34. Magee and other IRA terrorists had

In October 1984, the IRA terrorist group tried to assassinate British Prime Minister Margaret Thatcher and her cabinet by blowing up the Grand Hotel in Brighton, on England's south coast.

been trained at camps in Libya and brought their skills to Great Britain during a long campaign of terror and murder.

The technology did not exist then to track communications between the IRA, the KGB, and supply countries like Libya. It was known that other countries were involved in other atrocities carried out by terrorist groups such as the IRA and political groups in continental Europe. Many of these groups received funds from the Soviet Union and by sympathizers in other countries.

During the 1960s a protest group calling themselves the Baader Meinhof Gang arose in Germany. The group was a radical communist liberation movement, whose members became terrorists when they received funds and aid from the Soviet Union and worked with the IRA to spread terror across Europe through fire-bombings and murder.

Gerry Adams is the leader of Sinn Fein, the political wing of the IRA. In July 2002, the British government authorized the bugging of a car in which Adams was traveling. Here, he displays the listening equipment and digital-tracking device found in the car.

Long after the collapse of communism in the Soviet Union in the early 1990s, atrocities including the kidnapping and frequent murders of judges, company heads, and politicians continued under the name of this group. With public outrage and general disgust, there were increasing numbers of people willing to report their members to the police. Finally, on April 20, 1998, the gang sent a letter to the Reuters news agency saying that "Today we end this project. The urban guerrilla is dead."

The constant threat from terrorists since the end of World War II in 1945 has forced the development of technologies essential to tracking down terrorists. Spying and infiltration are not only about people putting themselves in the midst of these groups but also about eavesdropping and penetration of their communication channels. Sometimes, however, it is necessary for agents to pretend to join terrorist gangs to get names and contacts totally hidden from electronic spying. They have false backgrounds specially set up to appear genuine when checked. These agents have means of sending out messages but they exist in a world of lies, deceit, and a total absence of trust playing the role of a dedicated supporter of terror.

The fight against terrorism means some people have to operate from within camps, organized cells of criminals and to run the

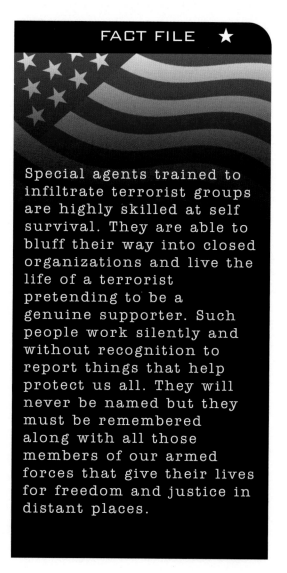

FACT FILE ★

Special agents trained to infiltrate terrorist groups are highly skilled at self survival. They are able to bluff their way into closed organizations and live the life of a terrorist pretending to be a genuine supporter. Such people work silently and without recognition to report things that help protect us all. They will never be named but they must be remembered along with all those members of our armed forces that give their lives for freedom and justice in distant places.

A street in Tehran, Iran, a country in President George W. Bush's "Axis of Evil" because it supports terrorism against the west. Western intelligence agents operating in countries like Iran face execution if they are ever caught.

risk every minute of exposure and a bullet in the head. These people work in countries known to supply terrorists with weapons, and they operate in banks that process money for attacks. These agents carry nothing on them that would give away their real intention but, unlike electronic devices, they are able to find members of terrorist gangs willing to defect and inform on their associates. This work is incredibly dangerous, because these people must find ways to bring the guilty to justice and to prevent yet another killing. Such is the ceaseless work of those who defend us from the menace of the terrorist.

Glossary

credible: a word describing something or someone considered trustworthy

efficiency: when something is carried out smoothly without any problems

electronic intelligence: intelligence gathered by electronic means from phone calls, e-mails, or faxes

espionage: the use of spies, often to gain military or political information

extremist: a person who has extreme political or religious views

freedom fighter: a person who takes part in violent action to overthrow an oppressive government

frequency-scanner: a device that scans radio frequencies to intercept electronic signals

geostationary: a geostationary satellite is one that travels at the same speed as the earth's rotation, which means it stays in the same place above the earth

guerrilla: a member of a small military group that carries out irregular fighting, often on larger forces

ideological: a word describing a system of ideas

infiltrating: when people or troops are sent to another country to spy and gain information

intelligence: secret information, often about an enemy group or country

liaison: a close working relationship among people, organizations, or countries

opposition party: a rival political party prepared to take power

recruitment: the act of joining a business or an organization such as the armed forces

sabotage: the deliberate destruction, damage, or obstruction of something to create difficulties for the enemy

signals-intelligence: a part of the military intelligence whose job it is to monitor radio and radar signals

totalitarian: a system of government that requires complete control over a state

transponder: a device used to receive radio signals and automatically transmit a different signal

Further Reading

Binns, Tristan. *The CIA (Government Agencies)*. Sagebrush, 2002

Binns, Tristan. *The FBI (Government Agencies)*. Sagebrush, 2002

Brennan, Kristine. *The Chernobyl Nuclear Disaster (Great Disasters)*. Chelsea House, 2002

Campbell, Geoffrey A. *A Vulnerable America (Lucent Library of Homeland Security)*. Lucent, 2003

Donovan, Sandra. *How Government Works: Protecting America*. Lerner Publishing Group, 2004

Gow, Mary. *Attack on America: The Day the Twin Towers Collapsed (American Disasters)*. Enslow Publishers, 2002

Hasan, Tahara. *Anthrax Attacks Around the World (Terrorist Attacks)*. Rosen Publishing Group, 2003

Katz, Samuel M. *Global Counterstrike: International Counterterrorism (Terrorist Dossiers)*. Lerner Publishing Group, 2004

Katz, Samuel M. *Targeting Terror: Counterterrorist Raids (Terrorist Dossiers)*. Lerner Publishing Group, 2004

Katz, Samuel M. *U.S. Counterstrike: American Counterterrorism (Terrorist Dossiers)*. Lerner Publishing Group, 2004

Margulies, Phillip. *Al-Qaeda: Osama Bin Laden's Army of Terrorists (Inside the World's Most Infamous Terrorist Organizations)*. Rosen Publishing Group, 2003

Marquette, Scott. *America Under Attack (America at War)*. Rourke Publishing LLC, 2003

Morris, Neil. *The Atlas of Islam*. Barron's, 2003

Owen, David. *Hidden Secrets: A Complete History of Espionage and the Technology Used to Support It*. Firefly Books Ltd, 2002

Ritchie, Jason. *Iraq and the Fall of Saddam Hussein*. Oliver Press, 2003

Websites to visit

The Central Intelligence Agency:
www.cia.gov

The Department of Defense:
www.defenselink.mil

The Department of Homeland Security:
www.dhs.gov

The Federal Bureau of Investigation:
www.fbi.gov

The U.S. Air Force:
www.af.mil

The U.S. Army
www.army.mil

The U.S. Coast Guard:
www.uscg.mil

The U.S. Government Official Website:
www.firstgov.gov

The U.S. Marine Corps:
www.usmc.mil

The U.S. Navy:
www.navy.mil

The U.S. Secret Service:
www.secretservice.gov

The White House:
www.whitehouse.gov

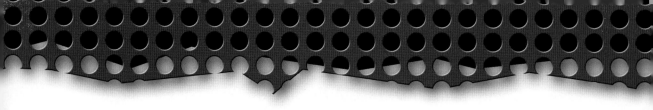

Index